To:

_____

From:

_____

May the God of hope fill you with
all joy and peace as you trust in him,
so that you may overflow with hope
by the power of the Holy Spirit.

Romans 15:13

footprints

inspirio™

INTRODUCTION

Every now and then during our devotional time my husband, Paul, and I reread the poem I wrote for him back in 1964. During these times of renewal and prayer, we talk over the events of our lives and share burdens we have for ourselves and others. Very often, we realize that the Great Shepherd has once again reached out and carried us through the day as we spend these introspective moments together.

If the pleasure of sharing these thoughts anew has taught us anything, it is this: that God's Word is true. Our Heavenly Father is faithful and will never leave us or forsake us. As we come to him daily, willing to be shaped and directed, his Word gives guideposts of clear direction. Almost everything we read, see, and experience shows us in some way that, although we do not visibly see God, he is with us. Over centuries of time others have looked back to understand that God's Spirit and presence were there, even when they felt alone.

In our quiet moments of reflection, in the fellowship of others and even in dreams, God opens the doors to our hearts. This is what happened when I originally wrote the poem, "Footprints."

After hours of wrestling with the darkness of doubt and despair, I finally surrendered to him and, in the early morning light of peace, wrote the poem as result of that spiritual experience.

Listen for the gentle stirring of God's grace in your own mind and soul as you read these verses of encouragement. Each of us is different in our spiritual need, just as each of our days is different. God wants to place his signature on your life in a unique way. As you spend time, even just a few moments each day, reflecting on his Word, it will help you to know him better.

Spiritual growth is not so much what we have done, but the feeling of love for him we put into everything we do. It is not so much in knowing about God that we grow, but in getting to know him in a personal, relational way. It is in becoming "a friend of God" as Abraham did that we grow in his grace, talking with him as our companion along the way letting God sift our thoughts and plans through the standards of his Word. May these verses encourage you anew each day as you walk with him.

Margaret Fishback Powers

Footprints

One night I dreamed a dream.
I was walking along the beach with my Lord.
Across the dark sky flashed scenes from my life.
For each scene, I noticed two sets of footprints in the sand,
one belonging to me and one to my Lord.
When the last scene of my life shot before me
I looked back at the footprints in the sand
and to my surprise,
I noticed that many times along the path of my life
there was only one set of footprints.
I realized that this was at the lowest and saddest times of my life.
This always bothered me
and I questioned the Lord
about my dilemma.
"Lord, you told me when I decided to follow You,
You would walk and talk with me all the way.
But I'm aware that during the most troublesome
times of my life there is only one set of footprints.
I just don't understand why, when I needed You most,
You leave me."
He whispered, "My precious child,
I love you and will never leave you
never, ever, during your trials and testings.
When you saw only one set of footprints
it was then that I carried you."

God Is With Us ...
In Our Dreams

One night
I dreamed
a dream.

*S*ome of our dreams can have a powerful effect on us. All of us have, at one time or another, awaken laughing or fretful—and all because of a dream. The Bible tells us about many people who had dreams and visions that were given to them by God.

[Jacob] had a dream in which he saw a stairway resting on the earth, with its top reaching to heaven, and the angels of God were ascending and descending on it.

Genesis 28:12

At Gibeon the LORD appeared to Solomon during the night in a dream, and God said, "Ask for whatever you want me to give you."

1 Kings 3:5

An angel of the Lord appeared to Joseph in a dream. "Get up," he said, "take the child [Jesus] and his mother and escape to Egypt. Stay there until I tell you, for Herod is going to search for the child to kill him."

Matthew 2:13

After Herod died, an angel of the Lord appeared in a dream to Joseph in Egypt and said, "Get up, take the child and his mother and go to the land of Israel, for those who were trying to take the child's life are dead."

Matthew 2:19–20

One day at about three in the afternoon [Cornelius] had a vision. He distinctly saw an angel of God, who came to him and said, "Cornelius! … Your prayers and gifts to the poor have come up as a memorial offering before God."

Acts 10:3

During the night Paul had a vision of a man of Macedonia standing and begging him, "Come over to Macedonia and help us."

Acts 16:9

*S*ome of our dreams are disappointing, but these are "wishful thinking" dreams, things we come up with in our own minds, circumstances or situations that we wish would happen. Only a small portion of these kind of dreams ever come true. In fact, these dreams can be harmful if we allow them to fill us with false hope.

This is what the LORD Almighty says:

"Do not listen to what the prophets are prophesying to you; they fill you with false hopes. They speak visions from their own minds, not from the mouth of the LORD."

Jeremiah 23:16

Yet we should not ignore our dreams. God will sometimes use our dreams to assure us of his promises or to tell us something about himself. And when God does speak to us in dreams, he will also help us understand them.

> God said, "Listen to my words:
> "When a prophet of the LORD is among you,
> I reveal myself to him in visions,
> I speak to him in dreams."
>
> Numbers 12:6

> "I will pour out my Spirit on all people.
> Your sons and daughters will prophesy,
> your old men will dream dreams,
> your young men will see visions," says the LORD.
>
> Joel 2:28

God's presence with us is no pipe dream. It is a reality. As we dream our dreams with the knowledge that God is with us, we will begin to see things as Christ does and dream dreams inspired by the Holy Spirit that are worth retelling and following.

God Is With Us …
In Our Daily Walk

I was walking
along the beach
with my Lord.

A close walk with the Lord is an important part of a believer's life.

God will teach us his ways,
so that we may walk in his paths.

Isaiah 2:3

May God turn our hearts to him, to walk in all his ways and to keep the commands, decrees and regulations he gave our fathers.

1 Kings 8:58

Your love is ever before me,
and I walk continually in your truth, LORD.

Psalm 26:3

He whose walk is upright fears the LORD.

Proverbs 14:2

The ways of the LORD are right;
the righteous walk in them.

Hosea 14:9

He whose walk is blameless is kept safe.

Proverbs 28:18

Let us walk in the light of the LORD.

Isaiah 2:5

*T*he Bible tells us that maintaining a close walk with God is a command we must obey, not merely a suggestion we may want to consider.

"I am God Almighty; walk before me and be blameless."

Genesis 17:1

What does the LORD your God ask of you but to fear the LORD your God, to walk in all his ways, to love him, to serve the LORD your God with all your heart and with all your soul.

Deuteronomy 10:12

Love the LORD your God … walk in all his ways … hold fast to him.

Deuteronomy 11:22

The LORD will establish you as his holy people, as he promised you on oath, if you keep the commands of the LORD your God and walk in his ways.

Deuteronomy 28:9

God has showed you, O man, what is good.
*And what does the L*ORD *require of you?*
To act justly and to love mercy
and to walk humbly with your God.

Micah 6:8

This is love: that we walk in obedience to God's commands. As you have heard from the beginning, his command is that you walk in love.

2 John 6

"Obey me, and I will be your God and you will be my people. Walk in all the ways I command you, that it may go well with you."

Jeremiah 7:23

Be very careful to keep the commandment and the law that Moses the servant of the LORD gave you: to love the LORD your God, to walk in all his ways, to obey his commands, to hold fast to him and to serve him with all your heart and all your soul.

Joshua 22:5

But what does a walk with God actually entail? How does God want us to live?

Love the LORD your God with all your heart and with all your soul and with all your strength. These commandments that I give you today are to be upon your hearts. Impress them on your children. Talk about them when you sit at home and when you walk along the road, when you lie down and when you get up.

Deuteronomy 6:5–7

He whose walk is blameless
and who does what is righteous,
who speaks the truth from his heart
and has no slander on his tongue,
who does his neighbor no wrong
and casts no slur on his fellowman,
who despises a vile man
but honors those who fear the LORD,
who keeps his oath
even when it hurts,
who lends his money without usury
and does not accept a bribe against the innocent.
He who does these things
will never be shaken.

Psalm 15:2–5

Many of these things that God asks us to do go against our nature. But the Bible urges us to consistently walk with the Lord, walking by faith, even when it's difficult.

> Live a life worthy of the LORD … please him in every way: bearing fruit in every good work, growing in the knowledge of God … giving thanks to the Father, who has qualified you to share in the inheritance of the saints in the kingdom of light.
>
> Colossians 1:10, 12

> Just as you received Christ Jesus as Lord, continue to live in him, rooted and built up in him, strengthened in the faith as you were taught, and overflowing with thankfulness.
>
> Colossians 2:6–7

> If we walk in the light, as God is in the light, we have fellowship with one another, and the blood of Jesus, his Son, purifies us from all sin.
>
> 1 John 1:7

Jesus said, "Walk while you have the light, before darkness overtakes you. The man who walks in the dark does not know where he is going. Put your trust in the light while you have it, so that you may become sons of light."

John 12:35–36

Live a life of love, just as Christ loved us.

Ephesians 5:2

Health professionals suggest that people who want to become physically fit should try a consistent program of walking. Sustained walking several times a week will improve your muscle tone and strengthen your heart.

The Bible reassures us that our spiritual lives will also reap benefits when we are consistent in walking with the Lord. Look at the many benefits a walk with God provides.

Walk in all the way that the LORD your God has commanded you, so that you may live and prosper and prolong your days in the land that you will possess.

Deuteronomy 5:33

When Jesus spoke again to the people, he said, "I am the light of the world. Whoever follows me will never walk in darkness, but will have the light of life."

John 8:12

He who walks righteously
and speaks what is right. …
this is the man who will dwell on the heights,
whose refuge will be the mountain fortress.
His bread will be supplied,
and water will not fail him.

Isaiah 33:15–16

The LORD God is a sun and shield;
the LORD bestows favor and honor;
no good thing does he withhold
from those whose walk is blameless.

Psalm 84:11

Blessed are they whose ways are blameless,
who walk according to the law of the LORD.
Blessed are they who keep his statutes
and seek him with all their heart.
They do nothing wrong;
they walk in his ways.

Psalm 119:1–3

God is a shield to those whose walk is blameless.

Proverbs 2:7

*Blessed are all who fear the L*ORD*,*
*   who walk in his ways.*
You will eat the fruit of your labor;
*   blessings and prosperity will be yours.*

Psalm 128:1–2

I guide you in the way of wisdom
*   and lead you along straight paths.*
When you walk, your steps will not be hampered;
*   when you run, you will not stumble.*

Proverbs 4:11–12

*Those who hope in the L*ORD *will renew their strength.*
They will soar on wings like eagles;
*   they will run and not grow weary,*
*   they will walk and not be faint.*

Isaiah 40:31

Blessed is the man
*   who does not walk in the counsel of the wicked*
or stand in the way of sinners
*   or sit in the seat of mockers.*
*But his delight is in the law of the L*ORD*,*
*   and on his law he meditates day and night.*
He is like a tree planted by streams of water,
*   which yields its fruit in season*
and whose leaf does not wither.
*   Whatever he does prospers.*

Psalm 1:1–3

We are the temple of the living God. As God has said: "I will live with them and walk among them, and I will be their God, and they will be my people."

2 Corinthians 6:16

This is what the LORD says:

> "Stand at the crossroads and look;
>   ask for the ancient paths,
> ask where the good way is, and walk in it,
>   and you will find rest for your souls."

Jeremiah 6:16

Fanny Crosby once said that the Lord "lovingly guards my footsteps and gives me songs in the night." A joyful heart is the mark of one who has a consistent walk with the Lord, who follows in the footsteps of the Master.

Take strength then, and be blessed in a close walk with the LORD, for "I will strengthen them in the LORD and in his name they will walk," declares the LORD (Zechariah 10:12).

God Is With Us ...
In the Hard Times

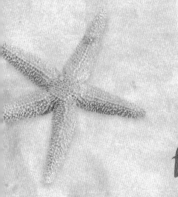

Across the
dark sky
flashed scenes
from my life.

*W*e all go through times when life seems to overwhelm us. The Bible reassures us that God's presence is with us to help us, even when we don't realize it.

> *God is our refuge and strength,*
> *an ever-present help in trouble.*

Psalm 46:1

> *In my distress I called to the LORD,*
> *and he answered me.*
> *From the depths of the grave I called for help,*
> *and you listened to my cry.*

Jonah 2:2

> *Those who know your name will trust in you,*
> *for you, LORD, have never forsaken those who seek you.*

Psalm 9:10

> *You are my hiding place, O LORD;*
> *you will protect me from trouble*
> *and surround me with songs of deliverance.*

Psalm 32:7

> *Even though I walk*
> *through the valley of the shadow of death,*
> *I will fear no evil,*
> *for you are with me;*
> *your rod and your staff,*
> *they comfort me.*

Psalm 23:4

My soul finds rest in God alone;
  my salvation comes from him.
He alone is my rock and my salvation;
  he is my fortress, I will never be shaken.

Psalm 62:1–2

Praise be to the LORD, to God our Savior,
  who daily bears our burdens.

Psalm 68:19

The LORD is my strength and my shield;
  my heart trusts in him, and I am helped.

Psalm 28:7

Moments of darkness in our lives may be caused by the death of a loved one, the loss of a job or a home or another great tragedy of life. Yet there is a greater darkness than these tragedies: the darkness in the eyes of one who has not felt God's love and grace and the assurance of his hope. There is hope for all of us. There is light. Jesus Christ, the Son of God, is our hope and light in darkness.

You are my lamp, O LORD;
  the LORD turns my darkness into light.

2 Samuel 22:29

You are a chosen people, a royal priesthood, a holy nation, a people belonging to God, that you may declare the praises of him who called you out of darkness into his wonderful light.

1 Peter 2:9

God is light; in him there is no darkness at all. If we claim to have fellowship with him yet walk in the darkness, we lie and do not live by the truth. But if we walk in the light, as he is in the light, we have fellowship with one another, and the blood of Jesus, his Son, purifies us from all sin.

1 John 1:5–7

In my distress I called to the LORD;
*   I called out to my God.*
From his temple he heard my voice;
*   my cry came to his ears … .*
He reached down from on high and took hold of me;
*   he drew me out of deep waters … .*
He brought me out into a spacious place;
*   he rescued me because he delighted in me.*

2 Samuel 22:7, 17, 20

Let him who walks in the dark,
*   who has no light,*
trust in the name of the LORD
*   and rely on his God.*

Isaiah 50:10

Jesus said, "I have come into the world as a light, so that no one who believes in me should stay in darkness."

John 12:46

Darkness covers the earth
        and thick darkness is over the peoples,
but the LORD rises upon you
        and his glory appears over you.

Isaiah 60:2

The LORD will be your everlasting light,
        and your God will be your glory.

Isaiah 60:19

        Though I have fallen, I will rise.
Though I sit in darkness,
        the LORD will be my light … .
He will bring me out into the light;
        I will see his righteousness.

Micah 7:8–9

Because of the tender mercy of our God …
        the rising sun will come to us from heaven
to shine on those living in darkness
        and in the shadow of death,
to guide our feet into the path of peace.

Luke 1:78–79

*O*ur dark times may also be a time when God wants to teach us something more about ourselves and his love for us. Our faith can be strengthened if we will wait patiently and trust God's heart-desire to make us more like himself.

> *A righteous man may have many troubles,*
> *   but the LORD delivers him from them all.*
>
> Psalm 34:19

> *Though you have made me see troubles, many and bitter,*
> *   you will restore my life again;*
> *from the depths of the earth*
> *   you will again bring me up, O LORD.*
>
> Psalm 71:20

We are hard pressed on every side, but not crushed; perplexed, but not in despair; persecuted, but not abandoned; struck down, but not destroyed. …We who are alive are always being given over to death for Jesus' sake, so that his life may be revealed in our mortal body.

2 Corinthians 4:8, 11

Our light and momentary troubles are achieving for us an eternal glory that far outweighs them all. So we fix our eyes not on what is seen, but on what is unseen. For what is seen is temporary, but what is unseen is eternal.

2 Corinthians 4:17–18

Be joyful in hope, patient in affliction, faithful in prayer.

Romans 12:12

Do not be surprised at the painful trial you are suffering, as though something strange were happening to you. But rejoice that you participate in the sufferings of Christ, so that you may be overjoyed when his glory is revealed.

1 Peter 4:12–13

Tragedy or testing, dark days or dreary nights, God knows what we are facing. He is in touch with what is happening to us, and he is concerned.

His eyes are on the ways of men;
he sees their every step.

Job 34:21

Jesus said, "In this world you will have trouble. But take heart! I have overcome the world."

John 16:33

Though I walk in the midst of trouble,
you preserve my life …
with your right hand you save me.

Psalm 138:7

God knows the way that I take;
when he has tested me, I will come forth as gold.

Job 23:10

I will be glad and rejoice in your love, O LORD,
for you saw my affliction
and knew the anguish of my soul.

Psalm 31:7

You discern my going out and my lying down;
you are familiar with all my ways.

Psalm 139:3

The LORD will keep you from all harm—
he will watch over your life;
the LORD will watch over your coming and going
both now and forevermore.

Psalm 121:7–8

"When you pass through the waters,
I will be with you;
and when you pass through the rivers,
they will not sweep over you.
When you walk through the fire,
you will not be burned;
the flames will not set you ablaze," says the LORD.

Isaiah 43:2–3

God Is With Us ...
As Our Companion

For each scene,
I noticed two sets
of footprints in the
sand, one belonging
to me and one
to my Lord.

I have a friend who loves to take long walks with me. We talk and laugh and enjoy each other's company as we stroll along. The exercise is beneficial, and so is the conversation.

The Lord is a lot like my friend. He enjoys walking with us as our companion on life's pathway. And he brings blessing into our lives when we walk closely with him.

> *"You will go out with joy*
> *and be led forth in peace;*
> *the mountains and hills*
> *will burst into song before you," says the Lord.*
>
> Isaiah 55:12

> *Blessed are those who have learned to acclaim you,*
> *who walk in the light of your presence.*
>
> Psalm 89:15

> *You have made known to me the path of life;*
> *you will fill me with joy in your presence,*
> *with eternal pleasures at your right hand.*
>
> Psalm 16:11

> "I will walk among you and be your God, and you will be my people," says the LORD.
>
> Leviticus 26:12

Two are better than one,
    because they have a good return for their work:
If one falls down,
    his friend can help him up.
But pity the man who falls
    and has no one to help him up!

Ecclesiastes 4:9–10

Blessed are all who fear the LORD,
    who walk in his ways.
You will eat the fruit of your labor;
    blessings and prosperity will be yours.

Psalm 128:1–2

Come ...
    let us walk in the light of the LORD.

Isaiah 2:5

Jesus said, "You are my friends if you do what I command. … I have called you friends, for everything that I learned from my Father I have made known to you."

John 15:14–15

*T*he awareness of God's presence with us is encouraging and heartwarming. It is as if we were two friends seated beside a rippling brook, enjoying a gentle breeze on a warm spring afternoon.

Jesus said, "Here I am! I stand at the door and knock. If anyone hears my voice and opens the door, I will come in and eat with him, and he with me."

Revelation 3:20

Come near to God and he will come near to you.

James 4:8

"Abraham believed God, and it was credited to him as righteousness," and he was called God's friend.

James 2:23

Jonathan said to David, "Go in peace, for we have sworn friendship with each other in the name of the LORD, saying, 'The LORD is witness between you and me, and between your descendants and my descendants forever.'"

1 Samuel 20:42

Even when we are surrounded by family and friends, some problems seem to double in size of their own accord. If we toss and turn in the early morning hours thinking about them, they become ten times as large. Yet though it seems the whole world has gone wrong around us, we are not alone—God is with us!

"So do not fear, for I am with you;
do not be dismayed, for I am your God.
I will strengthen you and help you;
I will uphold you with my righteous right hand."

Isaiah 41:10

Jesus said, "I will not leave you as orphans; I will come to you."

John 14:18

"For where two or three come together in my name, there am I with them," Jesus said.

Matthew 18:20

The eternal God is your refuge,
and underneath are the everlasting arms.

Deuteronomy 33:27

Who shall separate us from the love of Christ? Shall trouble or hardship or persecution or famine or nakedness or danger or sword? ... No, in all these things we are more than conquerors through him who loved us. For I am convinced that neither death nor life, neither angels nor demons, neither the present nor the future, nor any powers, neither height nor depth, nor anything else in all creation, will be able to separate us from the love of God that is in Christ Jesus our Lord.

Romans 8:35, 37–39

The LORD your God is a merciful God; he will not abandon or destroy you.

Deuteronomy 4:31

"Have I not commanded you? Be strong and courageous. Do not be terrified; do not be discouraged, for the LORD your God will be with you wherever you go," says the LORD.

Joshua 1:9

"Though the mountains be shaken
and the hills be removed,
yet my unfailing love for you will not be shaken
nor my covenant of peace be removed,"
says the LORD, who has compassion on you.

Isaiah 54:10

I will say of the LORD, "He is my refuge and my fortress,
my God, in whom I trust."

Psalm 91:2

"He will call upon me, and I will answer him;
I will be with him in trouble,
I will deliver him and honor him.
With long life will I satisfy him
and show him my salvation."

Psalm 91:15–16

Where can I go from your Spirit?
Where can I flee from your presence?
If I go up to the heavens, you are there;
if I make my bed in the depths, you are there.
If I rise on the wings of the dawn,
if I settle on the far side of the sea,
even there your hand will guide me,
your right hand will hold me fast.

Psalm 139:7–10

How great is your goodness,
which you have stored up for those who fear you,
which you bestow in the sight of men
on those who take refuge in you.

Psalm 31:19

God will not let your foot slip—
*   he who watches over you will not slumber. ...*
The LORD watches over you—
*   the LORD is your shade at your right hand;*
the sun will not harm you by day,
*   nor the moon by night.*
The LORD will keep you from all harm—
*   he will watch over your life;*
the LORD will watch over your coming and going
*   both now and forevermore.*

Psalm 121:3, 5–8

Jesus said, "I will come back and take you to be with me that you also may be where I am."

John 14:3

God has said,
*   "Never will I leave you;*
*   never will I forsake you."*

Hebrews 13:5

Wherever we go, we cannot step outside the boundaries of God's love and care. We can have fellowship "with the Father and with his Son, Jesus Christ" wherever we are (1 John 1:3). All we need to do is trust in God's loving companionship and walk the path he has placed before us.

God Is With Us . . .
Never Look Back!
No Regrets!

When the last
scene of my life
shot before me
I looked back
at the footprints
in the sand.

We say that hindsight is always 20/20. Looking back is something we often do but never consider the consequences of. However looking back is not recommended.

> Show me your ways, O LORD,
>   teach me your paths;
> guide me in your truth and teach me,
>   for you are God my Savior,
> and my hope is in you all day long.

Psalm 25:5

> Whoever invokes a blessing in the land
>   will do so by the God of truth
> he who takes an oath in the land
>   will swear by the God of truth.
> For the past troubles will be forgotten
>   and hidden from my eyes.
> Behold, I will create
>   new heavens and a new earth.
> The former things will not be remembered,
>   nor will they come to mind.

Isaiah 65:16–17

> Forget the former things;
>   do not dwell on the past.

Isaiah 43:18

Even the Lord Jesus reminded his listeners of the perils of looking back.

Jesus replied, "No one who puts his hand to the plow and looks back is fit for service in the kingdom of God."

Luke 9:62

When we live with an attitude that looks back over our lives with regrets and "if only's," we rob ourselves of hope. We rob ourselves of the joy of God's grace.

God has delivered us from such a deadly peril, and he will deliver us. On him we have set our hope that he will continue to deliver us.

2 Corinthians 1:10

What was glorious has no glory now in comparison with the surpassing glory. And if what was fading away came with glory, how much greater is the glory of that which lasts!

2 Corinthians 3:10–12

God never changes. He is the God of grace. He is the God of hope. He is the God of love who offers us a life free of regrets.

> Let us love one another, for love comes from God. Everyone who loves has been born of God and knows God. Whoever does not love does not know God, because God is love.
>
> 1 John 4:7–8

> *From everlasting to everlasting*
> *the LORD's love is with those who fear him,*
> *and his righteousness with their children's children—*
> *with those who keep his covenant*
> *and remember to obey his precepts.*
>
> Psalm 103:17–18

A life without regrets does not mean a life without repentance. When we sin, we must go beyond regretting and feeling sorry for our actions. We must move on to repentance by turning from our sinful ways and embracing God's forgiveness.

> Godly sorrow brings repentance that leads to salvation and leaves no regret.
>
> 2 Corinthians 7:10

> If anyone is in Christ, he is a new creation; the old has gone, the new has come!
>
> 2 Corinthians 5:17

Cleanse me with hyssop, and I will be clean;
     wash me, and I will be whiter than snow. ...
Hide your face from my sins
     and blot out all my iniquity.
Create in me a pure heart, O God,
     and renew a steadfast spirit within me.
Do not cast me from your presence
     or take your Holy Spirit from me.
Restore to me the joy of your salvation
     and grant me a willing spirit, to sustain me.

Psalm 51:7, 9–12

When we have experienced God's forgiveness, we are new creatures. We do not need to live a life of regrets, but rather we can live with a forward-looking hope of glory!

Forgetting what is behind and straining toward what is ahead, I press on toward the goal to win the prize for which God has called me heavenward in Christ Jesus.

Philippians 3:13–14

Let us throw off everything that hinders and the sin that so easily entangles, and let us run with perseverance the race marked out for us. Let us fix our eyes on Jesus, the author and perfecter of our faith.

Hebrews 12:1–2

I have fought the good fight, I have finished the race, I have kept the faith. Now there is in store for me the crown of righteousness, which the Lord, the righteous Judge, will award to me on that day—and not only to me, but also to all who have longed for his appearing.

2 Timothy 4:7–8

Whenever we do look back over our lives we must do so with God's perspective—no remorse or regrets. With God's perspective, we will be able to trace his hand on our lives and see that he has swept up the bad things of life and transformed them to good, just as he promised he would. With God's perspective, we will be able to live above regrets and live in God's peace and joy.

We know that in all things God works for the good of those who love him, who have been called according to his purpose.

Romans 8:28

Surely goodness and love will follow me
all the days of my life,
and I will dwell in the house of the LORD
forever.

Psalm 23:6

God Is With Us …
In Our Loneliness

And to my surprise,
I noticed that
many times
along the path
of my life
there was only one
set of footprints.

*T*oddlers often face separation anxiety—a feeling of abandonment whenever their parents leave the room. Though we may be much older and wiser than little children, we still feel the pain of loneliness and isolation. Both Jesus and the psalmist knew what it was to feel alone, abandoned and forgotten.

About the ninth hour Jesus cried out in a loud voice, "Eloi, Eloi, lama sabachthani?"—which means, "My God, my God, why have you forsaken me?"

Matthew 27:46

Do not hide your face from me,
> *do not turn your servant away in anger;*
> *you have been my helper.*
Do not reject me or forsake me,
> *O God my Savior.*

Psalm 27:9

I say to God my Rock,
> *"Why have you forgotten me?*
Why must I go about mourning,
> *oppressed by the enemy?"*

Psalm 42:9

My God, my God, why have you forsaken me?
> *Why are you so far from saving me,*
> *so far from the words of my groaning?*

Psalm 22:1

When we feel alone and abandoned, we can take comfort in God's promises to deliver us from our isolation and pain.

From the LORD comes deliverance.

Psalm 3:8

"The poor and needy search for water,
* but there is none;*
*   their tongues are parched with thirst.*
But I the LORD will answer them;
* I, the God of Israel, will not forsake them."*

Isaiah 41:17

"Can a mother forget the baby at her breast
* and have no compassion on the child she has borne?*
Though she may forget,
* I will not forget you!*
See, I have engraved you on the palms of my hands."

Isaiah 49:15–16

You are enthroned as the Holy One;
* you are the praise of Israel.*
In you our fathers put their trust;
* they trusted and you delivered them.*
They cried to you and were saved;
* in you they trusted and were not disappointed.*

Psalm 22:3–5

The LORD will not reject his people, because the LORD was pleased to make you his own.

1 Samuel 12:22

"So do not fear, for I am with you;
    do not be dismayed, for I am your God.
I will strengthen you and help you;
    I will uphold you with my righteous right hand."

Isaiah 41:10

Jesus said, "I will not leave you as orphans; I will come to you."

John 14:18

Keep me as the apple of your eye;
    Hide me in the shadow of your wings, O LORD.

Psalm 17:8

Wait for the LORD;
    be strong and take heart
    and wait for the LORD.

Psalm 27:14

Jesus said, "Do not let your hearts be troubled. Trust in God; trust also in me."

John 14:1

*How great is your goodness, O L*ORD*,*
        which you have stored up for those who fear you,
which you bestow in the sight of men
        on those who take refuge in you.
In the shelter of your presence you hide them ...
in your dwelling you keep them safe.

Psalm 31:19–20

He will not let your foot slip—
        he who watches over you will not slumber. ...
*The L*ORD *watches over you—*
        *the L*ORD *is your shade at your right hand;*
the sun will not harm you by day,
        nor the moon by night.
*The L*ORD *will keep you from all harm—*
        he will watch over your life;
*the L*ORD *will watch over your coming and going*
        both now and forevermore.

Psalm 121:3, 5–8

God is always with us—in our joy and in our pain, in the good times and in the bad times. His steadfast love and faithfulness are promises we can cling to, promises to bring us joy when we face loneliness.

"I will be with you; I will never leave you nor forsake you," says the LORD.

Joshua 1:5

Consider it pure joy whenever you face trials of many kinds, because you know that the testing of your faith develops perseverance. Perseverance must finish its work so that you may be made complete, not lacking anything.

James 1:2–4

Jesus said, "Surely I am with you always, to the very end of the age."

Matthew 28:20

Turn to me and have mercy on me,
*   as you always do to those who love your*
*   name, O LORD.*

Psalm 119:132

Be strong and courageous. Do not be afraid or terrified because of them, for the LORD your God goes with you; he will never leave you nor forsake you.

Deuteronomy 31:6

I will lie down and sleep in peace,
*   for you alone, O LORD, make me dwell in safety.*

Psalm 4:8

Where can I go from your Spirit?
Where can I flee from your presence?
If I go up to the heavens, you are there;
if I make my bed in the depths, you are there.
If I rise on the wings of the dawn,
if I settle on the far side of the sea,
even there your hand will guide me,
your right hand will hold me fast.

Psalm 139:7–10

David said about the Lord:
"I saw the Lord always before me.
Because he is at my right hand, I will not be shaken."

Acts 2:25

When loneliness overtakes us, we need to remember that we are not alone. God has promised to be with us. He will never forsake us. Lean on his promises and receive his peace.

Why are you downcast, O my soul?
Why so disturbed within me?
Put your hope in God,
for I will yet praise him,
my Savior and my God.

Psalm 42:11

Jesus said, "A new command I give you: Love one another. As I have loved you, so you must love one another. By this all men will know that you are my disciples, if you love one another."

John 13:34–35

Jesus said, "Whoever has my commands and obeys them, he is the one who loves me. He who loves me will be loved by my Father, and I too will love him and show myself to him."

John 14:21

Live a life of love, just as Christ loved us and gave himself up for us as a fragrant offering and sacrifice to God.

Ephesians 5:2

God Is With Us …
In Our Sorrow

I realized that
this was at
the lowest
and saddest
times of my life.

*S*orrow can cause us to doubt God's plan. The psalmist cried, "Has his unfailing love vanished forever? Has his promise failed for all time? Has God forgotten to be merciful? Has he in anger withheld his compassion?" (Psalm 77:8–9). Though we may face trouble and difficulties, sadness and pain, God is still in control, and he is always with us.

> *My flesh and my heart may fail,*
> *but God is the strength of my heart*
> *and my portion forever.*

Psalm 73:26

> *I love you, O LORD, my strength.*
> *The LORD is my rock, my fortress and my deliverer;*
> *my God is my rock, in whom I take refuge.*
> *He is my shield and the horn of my salvation, my stronghold.*

Psalm 18:1–2

> *When I said, "My foot is slipping,"*
> *your love, O LORD, supported me.*
> *When anxiety was great within me,*
> *your consolation brought joy to my soul.*

Psalm 94:18–19

> *The LORD upholds all those who fall*
> *and lifts up all who are bowed down.*

Psalm 145:14

The LORD is a refuge for the oppressed,
a stronghold in times of trouble.

Psalm 9:9

We must remember to listen closely to God's voice when trouble rages around us. When the agonies of life begin to crush us, God has not moved away from us. Often we have moved away from him. We need to return to him in faith and call on him for his strength.

I have put my trust in you, LORD.
Show me the way I should go,
for to you I lift up my soul.

Psalm 143:8

Return to the LORD your God,
for he is gracious and compassionate,
slow to anger and abounding in love.

Joel 2:13

If the LORD delights in a man's way,
he makes his steps firm;
though he stumble, he will not fall,
for the LORD upholds him with his hand.

Psalm 37:23–24

I sought the LORD, and he answered me;
he delivered me from all my fears.

Psalm 34:4

My soul finds rest in God alone;
*   my salvation comes from him.*
He alone is my rock and my salvation;
*   he is my fortress, I will never be shaken.*

Psalm 62:1–2

Surely, O LORD, you bless the righteous;
*   you surround them with your favor as with a shield.*

Psalm 5:12

Jesus said, "Peace I leave with you; my peace I give you. I do not give to you as the world gives. Do not let your hearts be troubled and do not be afraid."

John 14:27

"I have told you these things, so that in me you may have peace. In this world you will have trouble. But take heart! I have overcome the world."

John 16:33

Jesus said, "My grace is sufficient for you, for my power is made perfect in weakness."

2 Corinthians 12:9

We who have fled to take hold of the hope offered to us may be greatly encouraged. We have this hope as an anchor for the soul, firm and secure.

Hebrews 6:18–19

Praise be to the God and Father of our Lord Jesus Christ, the Father of compassion and the God of all comfort, who comforts us in all our troubles, so that we can comfort those in any trouble with the comfort we ourselves have received from God.

2 Corinthians 1:3–4

"As a mother comforts her child,
so will I comfort you," … says the LORD.
When you see this, your heart will rejoice
and you will flourish like grass;
the hand of the LORD *will be made known to his servants.*

Isaiah 66:13–14

My comfort in my suffering is this:
Your promise preserves my life, LORD.

Psalm 119:50

We do not have a high priest who is unable to sympathize with our weaknesses, but we have one who has been tempted in every way, just as we are—yet was without sin. Let us then approach the throne of grace with confidence, so that we may receive mercy and find grace to help us in our time of need.

Hebrews 4:15–16

*J*esus experienced sorrow of the deepest kind in the Garden of Gethsemane—the sorrow of impending death. We also experience pain when death takes a loved one, but God reminds us that he is still in control. Death is not the master— God is.

> For none of us lives to himself alone and none of us dies to himself alone. If we live, we live to the Lord; and if we die, we die to the Lord. So, whether we live or die, we belong to the Lord.
>
> Romans 14:7–8

> If only for this life we have hope in Christ, we are to be pitied more than all men. But Christ has indeed been raised from the dead. ... Since death came through a man, the resurrection of the dead comes also through a man. For as in Adam all die, so in Christ all will be made alive.
>
> 1 Corinthians 15:19–22

> Listen, I tell you a mystery: We will not all sleep, but we will all be changed—in a flash, in the twinkling of an eye, at the last trumpet. For the trumpet will sound, the dead will be raised imperishable, and we will be changed.
>
> 1 Corinthians 15:51–52

Even though I walk
through the valley of the shadow of death,
I will fear no evil,
for you are with me;
your rod and your staff,
they comfort me.

Psalm 23:4

We believe that Jesus died and rose again and so we believe that God will bring with Jesus those who have fallen asleep in him. … For the Lord himself will come down from heaven, with a loud command, with the voice of the archangel and with the trumpet call of God, and the dead in Christ will rise first. After that, we who are still alive and are left will be caught up together with them in the clouds to meet the Lord in the air. And so we will be with the Lord forever.

1 Thessalonians 4:14, 16–17

To live is Christ and to die is gain.

Philippians 1:21

Jesus said, "Do not let your hearts be troubled. Trust in God; trust also in me. In my Father's house are many rooms; if it were not so, I would have told you. I am going there to prepare a place for you. And if I go and prepare a place for you, I will come back and take you to be with me that you also may be where I am. You know the way to the place where I am going."

John 14:1–4

Whether we face death, discouragement, loss or pain, we can take great comfort in knowing that no sorrow is too deep that God cannot feel it with us. And God wants to help deliver us from it. He wants to bring us his divine comfort.

This I call to mind
* and therefore I have hope:*
Because of the LORD's great love we are not consumed,
* for his compassions never fail.*
They are new every morning;
* great is your faithfulness.*

Lamentations 3:21–23

The LORD is good to those whose hope is in him,
* to the one who seeks him.*

Lamentations 3:25

Cast your cares on the LORD
* and he will sustain you;*
* he will never let the righteous fall.*

Psalm 55:22

Do not be anxious about anything, but in everything, by prayer and petition, with thanksgiving, present your requests to God. And the peace of God, which transcends all understanding, will guard your hearts and your minds in Christ Jesus.

Philippians 4:6–7

God gives strength to the weary
and increases the power of the weak.
Even youths grow tired and weary,
and young men stumble and fall.
but those who hope in the LORD
will renew their strength.
They will soar on wings like eagles;
they will run and not grow weary,
they will walk and not be faint.

Isaiah 40:29–30

"For I am the LORD, your God,
who takes hold of your right hand
and says to you, Do not fear;
I will help you."

Isaiah 41:13

In all their distress [the Messiah] too was distressed,
and the angel of his presence saved them.
In his love and mercy he redeemed them;
he lifted them up and carried them.

Isaiah 63:9

Jesus said, "Come to me, all you who are weary and burdened, and I will give you rest. Take my yoke upon you and learn from me, for I am gentle and humble in heart, and you will find rest for your souls."

Matthew 11:28–29

Shout for joy, O heavens;
rejoice, O earth;
burst into song, O mountains!
For the LORD comforts his people
and will have compassion on his afflicted ones.

Isaiah 49:13

"I will refresh the weary and satisfy the faint,"
says the LORD.

Jeremiah 31:25

The ransomed of the LORD will return.
they will enter Zion with singing;
everlasting joy will crown their heads.
Gladness and joy will overtake them,
and sorrow and sighing will flee away.
"I, even I, am he who comforts you," says the LORD.

Isaiah 51:11–12

Though things may seem hopeless, God, who has called you into fellowship with his Son Jesus Christ our Lord, is faithful (1 Corinthians 1:9). No trial is so great that God cannot deliver us. No pain is so great that he does not bring us comfort. And no situation is ever without God's presence.

God Is With Us ...
Why Should We Fret?

This always bothered me ...

Fretting and a kitchen blender have a lot in common. With the push of a button the contents of a blender are whirled and swirled until they become a frothy, churned mixture. In our lives, fretting chews and gnaws and wears away at us until our lives become a churned jumble. But God doesn't want us to live "blender-ized" lives of fretting.

> Do not fret because of evil men
>   or be envious of those who do wrong;
> for like the grass they will soon wither,
>   like green plants they will soon die away.
> Trust in the LORD and do good.
>
> Psalm 37:1–3

> Be still before the LORD and wait patiently for him.
>
> Psalm 37:7

> God did not give us a spirit of timidity, but a spirit of power, of love and of self-discipline.
>
> 2 Timothy 1:7

Fretting easily leads to worry; worry casts a big shadow over small problems—a shadow that should never cross our lives.

> Jesus said, "Do not worry about your life, what you will eat; or about your body, what you will wear. Life is more than food, and the body more than clothes."
>
> Luke 12:22–23

Jesus said, "Who of you by worrying can add a single hour to his life? And why do you worry about clothes? See how the lilies of the field grow. They do not labor or spin. Yet I tell you that not even Solomon in all his splendor was dressed like one of these. If that is how God clothes the grass of the field, which is here today and tomorrow is thrown into the fire, will he not much more clothe you?"

Matthew 6:27–30

*W*hen the outlook is not good, we should not fret. We need a change of perspective to realize that God sees tomorrow more clearly than we see yesterday. We don't need to fret! The future is completely in his hands!

"I am concerned for you and will look on you with favor," says the LORD.

Ezekiel 36:9

Commit to the LORD whatever you do,
and your plans will succeed.

Proverbs 16:3

Jesus said, "Do not worry, saying, 'What shall we eat?' or 'What shall we drink?' or 'What shall we wear?'… Seek first his kingdom and his righteousness, and all these things will be given to you as well."

Matthew 6:31, 33

Don't fret! Cheer up! Neither the sun, nor the Son, have gone out of business. He is with us. A new day will dawn, and the Lord will bring himself to the center of our problems.

> Blessed is the man who trusts in the LORD,
>   whose confidence is in him.
> He will be like a tree planted by the water
>   that sends out its roots by the stream.
> It does not fear when heat comes;
>   its leaves are always green.
> It has no worries in a year of drought
>   and never fails to bear fruit.
>
> Jeremiah 17:7–8

Because of his great love for us, God, who is rich in mercy, made us alive with Christ.

> Ephesians 2:4–5

> Seek the LORD while he may be found;
>   call on him while he is near.
>
> Isaiah 55:6

> My flesh and my heart may fail,
>   but God is the strength of my heart
>   and my portion forever.
>
> Psalm 73:26

He who fears the LORD has a secure fortress.

Proverbs 14:26

Great peace have they who love your law, O LORD,
and nothing can make them stumble.

Psalm 119:165

God has said, "Never will I leave you; never will I forsake you." So we say with confidence, "The Lord is my helper; I will not be afraid. What can man do to me?"

Hebrews 13:5–6

The LORD himself goes before you and will be with you; he will never leave you nor forsake you. Do not be afraid; do not be discouraged.

Deuteronomy 31:8

The LORD heals the brokenhearted
and binds up their wounds.

Psalm 147:3

Jesus said, "Are not five sparrows sold for two pennies? Yet not one of them is forgotten by God. Indeed, the very hairs of your head are all numbered. Don't be afraid; you are worth more than many sparrows."

Luke 12:6–7

Remember, fretting will only tie us in knots. Prayer is the only way to shortcut our fretting—to cut those knots of worry and care and grant us God's peace instead.

> Do not be anxious about anything, but in everything, by prayer and petition, with thanksgiving, present your requests to God. And the peace of God, which transcends all understanding, will guard your hearts and your minds in Christ Jesus.
>
> Philippians 4:6–7

God Is With Us …
When We Need Direction

And I questioned
the Lord
about my
dilemma.

When a transit strike brought our recently purchased business to a standstill, I found myself wondering if we had made the right decision to get into this new business. The choice seemed to be the right one at the time, but now I wasn't so sure. How was I supposed to sort out what we should do next? When we face questions of this kind, we need to get our arms around God's wisdom.

If any of you lacks wisdom, he should ask God, who gives generously to all without finding fault, and it will be given to him.

James 1:5

"I will instruct you and teach you in the way you should go;
I will counsel you and watch over you," says the LORD.

Psalm 32:8

Trust in the LORD with all your heart
and lean not on your own understanding;
in all your ways acknowledge him,
and he will make your paths straight.

Proverbs 3:5–6

The way of a fool seems right to him,
but a wise man listens to advice.

Proverbs 12:15

The LORD will guide you always;
he will satisfy your needs in a sun-scorched land
and will strengthen your frame.
You will be like a well-watered garden,
like a spring whose waters never fail.

Isaiah 58:11

Jesus said, "When he, the Spirit of truth, comes, he will guide you into all truth. He will not speak on his own; he will speak only what he hears, and he will tell you what is yet to come."

John 16:13

Show me your ways, O LORD,
teach me your paths;
guide me in your truth and teach me,
for you are God my Savior,
and my hope is in you all day long.

Psalm 25:4–5

This is what the LORD says—
your Redeemer, the Holy One of Israel:
"I am the LORD your God,
who teaches you what is best for you,
who directs you in the way you should go."

Isaiah 48:17

Wisdom is supreme; therefore get wisdom.
Though it cost all you have, get understanding.

Proverbs 4:7

God doesn't mind our questions when we come to him with a seeking heart. God is bigger than any question we can ask. And he often will give us the answers we seek in his Word.

> *Your word is a lamp to my feet*
> *and a light for my path.*

Psalm 119:105

> *These commands are a lamp,*
> *this teaching is a light,*
> *and the corrections of discipline*
> *are the way to life.*

Proverbs 6:23

Do not let this Book of the Law depart from your mouth; meditate on it day and night, so that you may be careful to do everything written in it. Then you will be prosperous and successful.

Joshua 1:8

> *Pay attention and listen to the sayings of the wise;*
> *apply your heart to what I teach,*
> *for it is pleasing when you keep them in your heart*
> *and have all of them ready on your lips.*

Proverbs 22:17–18

*W*hen we find ourselves questioning God's reason for allowing certain things to happen, we must stop, remember God's faithfulness and depend upon his grace. Whatever our questions, whatever our circumstances, God is still in control.

Know therefore that the LORD your God is God; he is the faithful God, keeping his covenant of love to a thousand generations of those who love him and keep his commands.

Deuteronomy 7:9

Since you are my rock and my fortress,
for the sake of your name lead and guide me.

Psalm 31:3

Great is your love, O God, higher than the heavens;
your faithfulness reaches to the skies.

Psalm 108:4

The LORD will fulfill his purpose for me;
your love, O LORD, endures forever—
do not abandon the works of your hands.

Psalm 138:8

*Let us acknowledge the L*ORD*;*
*   let us press on to acknowledge him.*
As surely as the sun rises,
*   he will appear;*
he will come to us like the winter rains,
*   like the spring rains that water the earth.*

Hosea 6:3

God is our God forever and ever;
*   he will be our guide even to the end.*

Psalm 48:14

When we need direction, we must trust that the Lord will take our faith, limited as it is, and make something of lasting value out of it. God has a plan for us. He cares about our dilemmas, hears our heartfelt cries and will answer us in ways that will astonish us and fill our hearts with songs of joy.

"I know the plans I have for you," declares the LORD, "plans to prosper you and not to harm you, plans to give you hope and a future."

Jeremiah 29:11

God Is With Us …
In Our Decisions

"Lord, you
told me when
I decided to
follow You..."

It seems that sometimes all we do is make decisions. Some come quickly without much thought, others take more time and consideration. How can God help us?

> I guide you in the way of wisdom
> and lead you along straight paths.

Proverbs 4:11

> Trust in the LORD with all your heart
> and lean not on your own understanding;
> in all your ways acknowledge him,
> and he will make your paths straight.
> Do not be wise in your own eyes.
> fear the LORD and shun evil.
> This will bring health to your body
> and nourishment to your bones.

Proverbs 3:5–8

> Do you not know?
> Have you not heard?
> The LORD is the everlasting God,
> the Creator of the ends of the earth.
> He will not grow tired or weary,
> and his understanding no one can fathom.

Isaiah 40:28

I know whom I have believed, and am convinced that God is able to guard what I have entrusted to him for that day.

2 Timothy 1:12

Where then does wisdom come from?
Where does understanding dwell?
It is hidden from the eyes of every living thing,
concealed even from the birds of the air. ...
God understands the way to it
and he alone knows where it dwells.

Job 28:20–21, 23

"Have faith in God," Jesus [said]. "I tell you the truth, if anyone says to this mountain, 'Go, throw yourself into the sea, and does not doubt in his heart but believes that what he says will happen, it will be done for him. Therefore, I tell you, whatever you ask for in prayer, believe that you have received it, and it will be yours."

Mark 11:22–24

The decisions we need to make may be simple or they may be complex, but they should always be predicated on our decision to follow the Lord.

Listen, my son, accept what I say,
and the years of your life will be many.
I guide you in the way of wisdom
and lead you along straight paths.
When you walk, your steps will not be hampered;
when you run, you will not stumble.

Proverbs 4:10–12

Fear the LORD and serve him faithfully with all your heart; consider what great things he has done for you.

1 Samuel 12:24

Jesus said, "Whoever acknowledges me before men, I will also acknowledge him before my Father in heaven."

Matthew 10:32

Choose for yourselves this day whom you will serve. … As for me and my household, we will serve the LORD.

Joshua 24:15

Whatever you do, work at it with all your heart, as working for the Lord, not for men, since you know that you will receive an inheritance from the Lord as a reward. It is the Lord Christ you are serving.

Colossians 3:23–24

It is the LORD your God you must follow, and him you must revere. Keep his commands and obey him; serve him and hold fast to him.

Deuteronomy 13:4

When we decide to follow the Lord, it means we must live our lives the way he wants us to, following his commands, yielded to his control.

Those who live according to the sinful nature have their minds set on what that nature desires; but those who live in accordance with the Spirit have their minds set on what the Spirit desires.

Romans 8:5

The one who sows to please his sinful nature, from that nature will reap destruction; the one who sows to please the Spirit, from the Spirit will reap eternal life.

Galatians 6:8

My son, keep your father's commands
and do not forsake your mother's teaching.
Bind them upon your heart forever;
fasten them around your neck.
When you walk, they will guide you;
when you sleep, they will watch over you;
when you awake, they will speak to you.

Proverbs 6:20–22

The grace of God that brings salvation has appeared to all men. It teaches us to say "No" to ungodliness and worldly passions, and to live self-controlled, upright and godly lives in this present age.

Titus 2:11–12

Make every effort to live in peace with all men and to be holy.

Hebrews 12:14

Offer your bodies as living sacrifices, holy and pleasing to God—this is your spiritual act of worship. Do not conform any longer to the pattern of this world, but be transformed by the renewing of your mind.

Romans 12:1–2

God did not call us to be impure, but to live a holy life.

1 Thessalonians 4:7

Never be lacking in zeal, but keep your spiritual fervor, serving the Lord.

Romans 12:11

Prepare your minds for action; be self-controlled; set your hope fully on the grace to be given you when Jesus Christ is revealed.

1 Peter 1:13

Serve God with wholehearted devotion and with a willing mind, for the LORD searches every heart and understands every motive behind the thoughts.

1 Chronicles 28:9

Now that you have been set free from sin and have become slaves to God, the benefit you reap leads to holiness, and the result is eternal life.

Romans 6:22

Let us purify ourselves from everything that contaminates body and spirit, perfecting holiness out of reverence for God.

2 Corinthians 7:1

Just as God who called you is holy, so be holy in all you do; for it is written: "Be holy, because I am holy."

1 Peter 1:15–16

Just as you received Christ Jesus as Lord, continue to live in him, rooted and built up in him, strengthened in the faith as you were taught, and overflowing with thankfulness.

Colossians 2:6–7

Pursue righteousness, godliness, faith, love, endurance and gentleness. Fight the good fight of the faith.

1 Timothy 6:11–12

Do not turn away from the LORD, but serve the LORD with all your heart.

1 Samuel 12:20

Let your eyes look straight ahead,
*   fix your gaze directly before you.*
Make level paths for your feet
*   and take only ways that are firm.*

Proverbs 4:25–26

Let us hold unswervingly to the hope we profess, for he who promised is faithful.

Hebrews 10:23

Since we are surrounded by such a great cloud of witnesses, let us throw off everything that hinders and the sin that so easily entangles, and let us run with perseverance the race marked out for us.

Hebrews 12:1

LORD, who may dwell in your sanctuary?
*   Who may live on your holy hill?*
He whose walk is blameless
*   and who does what is righteous,*
who speaks the truth from his heart.

Psalm 15:1–2

This is how we know who the children of God are and who the children of the devil are: Anyone who does not do what is right is not a child of God; nor is anyone who does not love his brother.

1 John 3:10

"He follows my decrees
and faithfully keeps my laws.
That man is righteous;
he will surely live,"
declares the Sovereign LORD.

Ezekiel 18:9

Let the word of Christ dwell in you richly as you teach and admonish one another with all wisdom, and as you sing psalms, hymns and spiritual songs with gratitude in your hearts to God. And whatever you do, whether in word or deed, do it all in the name of the Lord Jesus, giving thanks to God the Father through him.

Colossians 3:16–17

Jesus said, "Blessed ... are those who hear the word of God and obey it."

Luke 11:28

We all need God's divine power from day to day to follow in his footsteps—to learn the eternal, upside-down, inside-out values of God's kingdom so that we may make decisions based on his character and ultimately share in his glory.

If anyone speaks, he should do it as one speaking the very words of God. If anyone serves, he should do it with the strength God provides, so that in all things God may be praised through Jesus Christ.

1 Peter 4:11

God Is With Us ...
As Our Guide

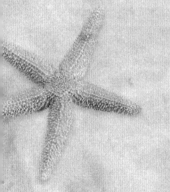

"You would
walk and talk
with me
all the way."

I saw two children walking together today, happily exchanging words and glances, laughing aloud at shared jokes. They didn't worry about the cracks in the sidewalk or the bumps in the road, but rather skipped along over them. God wants our walk with him to be just like that—enjoying his company, sharing together and crossing the rough places on our journey home without the slightest care.

May the nations be glad and sing for joy,
for you rule the peoples justly
and guide the nations of the earth.

Psalm 67:4

"I will lead the blind by ways they have not known,
along unfamiliar paths I will guide them;
I will turn the darkness into light before them
and make the rough places smooth.
These are the things I will do;
I will not forsake them."

Isaiah 42:16

Because of your great compassion you did not abandon them in the desert. By day the pillar of cloud did not cease to guide them on their path, nor the pillar of fire by night to shine on the way they were to take. You gave your good Spirit to instruct them.

Nehemiah 9:19–20

The integrity of the upright guides them.

Proverbs 11:3

The LORD gives sight to the blind,
the LORD lifts up those who are bowed down,
the LORD loves the righteous.

Psalm 146:8

You have delivered me from death
and my feet from stumbling,
that I may walk before God
in the light of life.

Psalm 56:13

The LORD guards the course of the just
and protects the way of his faithful ones.

Proverbs 2:8

Many times along our life-walk the path becomes obscure. We need someone to help show us the way. That someone is God.

In your unfailing love you will lead
the people you have redeemed, O LORD.
In your strength your will guide them
to your holy dwelling.

Exodus 15:13

God guides the humble in what is right
and teaches them his way.

Psalm 25:9

The LORD guides me in paths of righteousness
    for his name's sake.

Psalm 23:3

You guide me with your counsel, LORD,
    and afterward you will take me into glory.

Psalm 73:24

In his heart a man plans his course,
    but the LORD determines his steps.

Proverbs 16:9

Since you are my rock and my fortress,
    for the sake of your name lead and guide me.

Psalm 31:3

Show me your ways, O LORD,
    teach me your paths;
guide me in your truth and teach me,
    for you are God my Savior,
    and my hope is in you all day long.

Psalm 25:4–5

Teach me your way, O LORD;
lead me in a straight path.

Psalm 27:11

The path of the righteous is like the first gleam of dawn,
shining ever brighter till the full light of day.

Proverbs 4:18

Lead me, O LORD, in your righteousness …
make straight your way before me.

Psalm 5:8

I will praise the LORD, who counsels me;
even at night my heart instructs me.

Psalm 16:7

Teach me to do your will,
for you are my God;
may your good Spirit
lead me on level ground.

Psalm 143:10

God who has compassion on [the captives] will guide them
and lead them beside springs of water.

Isaiah 49:10

Ｇod's Word becomes our road map for our daily walk with the Savior.

Jesus said, "If you hold to my teaching, you are really my disciples. Then you will know the truth, and the truth will set you free."

John 8:31–32

The precepts of the LORD are right,
*   giving joy to the heart.*
The commands of the LORD are radiant,
*   giving light to the eyes.*

Psalm 19:8–9

Ｈis Word reminds us of his power, his provision and his sovereignty.

You are awesome, O God, in your sanctuary;
*   the God of Israel gives power and strength to his people.*

Psalm 68:35

Great is our LORD and mighty in power;
*   his understanding has no limit.*

Psalm 147:5

To God belong wisdom and power;
*   counsel and understanding are his.*

Job 12:13

Keep the LORD's decrees and commands, which I am giving you today, so that it may go well with you and your children after you and that you may live long in the land the LORD your God gives you for all time.

Deuteronomy 4:40

His Word reminds us of his love.

Jesus said, "As the Father has loved me, so have I loved you. Now remain in my love."

John 15:9

Therefore, as God's chosen people, holy and dearly loved, clothe yourselves with compassion, kindness, humility, gentleness and patience. Bear with each other and forgive whatever grievances you may have against one another. Forgive as the Lord forgave you. And over all these virtues put on love, which binds them all together in perfect unity.

Colossians 3:12–14

The Lord appeared to us in the past, saying:

*"I have loved you with an everlasting love;
I have drawn you with loving-kindness."*

Jeremiah 31:3

How great is the love the Father has lavished on us, that we should be called children of God!

1 John 3:1

Let's enjoy the time with God as he walks and talks with us each day, wherever we are.

I pray that out of his glorious riches he may strengthen you with power through his Spirit in your inner being, so that Christ may dwell in your hearts through faith. And I pray that you, being rooted and established in love, may have power, together with all the saints, to grasp how wide and long and high and deep is the love of Christ, and to know this love that surpasses knowledge—that you may be filled to the measure of all the fullness of God.

Ephesians 3:16–19

"Be still, and know that I am God;
I will be exalted among the nations,
I will be exalted in the earth."
The LORD Almighty is with us;
the God of Jacob is our fortress.

Psalm 46:10–11

God Is With Us . . .
In Our Difficulties

"But I'm aware
that during the
most troublesome
times of my life
there is only
one set of
footprints."

Ruts and potholes. Shadows and deep darkness. The journey of life can sometimes be very troubling. We stumble and have difficulty following in God's footsteps. We are fearful of the unknown. But God's Word reminds us to trust, to believe, to hope.

> *Now, LORD, what do I look for?*
>   *My hope is in you.*

Psalm 39:7

Everyone born of God overcomes the world. This is the victory that has overcome the world, even our faith. Who is it that overcomes the world? Only he who believes that Jesus is the Son of God.

1 John 5:4–5

> *Put your hope in the LORD,*
>   *for with the LORD is unfailing love*
>   *and with him is full redemption.*

Psalm 130:7

> *Blessed is he whose help is the God of Jacob,*
>   *whose hope is in the LORD his God,*
> *the Maker of heaven and earth,*
>   *the sea, and everything in them—*
>   *the LORD, who remains faithful forever.*

Psalm 146:5–6

Everything that was written in the past was written to teach us, so that through endurance and the encouragement of the Scriptures we might have hope.

Romans 15:4

Faith is being sure of what we hope for and certain of what we do not see.

Hebrews 11:1

Praise be to the God and Father of our Lord Jesus Christ! In his great mercy he has given us new birth into a living hope through the resurrection of Jesus Christ from the dead.

1 Peter 1:3

When I am afraid,
I will trust in you.
In God, whose word I praise,
in God I trust; I will not be afraid.
What can mortal man do to me?

Psalm 56:3–4

As for me, I watch in hope for the LORD,
I wait for God my Savior;
my God will hear me.

Micah 7:7

We all go through troubling times, but we must never doubt God's presence with us.

You are a forgiving God, gracious and compassionate, slow to anger and abounding in love.

Nehemiah 9:17

As a father has compassion on his children,
so the LORD has compassion on those who fear him.

Psalm 103:13

Your love, O LORD, reaches to the heavens,
your faithfulness to the skies.

Psalm 36:5

The LORD your God is a merciful God; he will not abandon or destroy you.

Deuteronomy 4:31

"I will betroth you to me forever;
I will betroth you in righteousness and justice,
in love and compassion," declares the LORD.

Hosea 2:19

God has poured out his love into our hearts by the Holy Spirit, whom he has given us.

Romans 5:5

*G*od will never let us down. He promises us his strength, his peace, his comfort and his presence. All we need to do is depend on him, for we can never break God's promises by leaning on them.

Do not be afraid. Stand firm and you will see the deliverance the LORD will bring you today. … The LORD will fight for you; you need only to be still.

Exodus 14:13–14

He who dwells in the shelter of the Most High
will rest in the shadow of the Almighty.
I will say of the LORD, "He is my refuge and my fortress,
my God, in whom I trust."

Psalm 91:1–2

The LORD longs to be gracious to you;
he rises to show you compassion.

Isaiah 30:18

The plans of the LORD stand firm forever,
the purposes of his heart through all generations.

Psalm 33:11

Evening, morning and noon
I cry out in distress,
and he hears my voice.

Psalm 55:17

The eyes of the LORD range throughout the earth to strengthen those whose hearts are fully committed to him.

2 Chronicles 16:9

I wait for you, O LORD;
you will answer, O Lord my God.

Psalm 38:15

You will call, and the LORD will answer;
you will cry for help, and he will say: Here am I.

Isaiah 58:9

"Call upon me in the day of trouble;
I will deliver you, and you will honor me."

Psalm 50:15

May you be richly rewarded by the LORD, the God of Israel, under whose wings you have come to take refuge.

Ruth 2:12

It is God who arms me with strength
and makes my way perfect.
He makes my feet like the feet of a deer;
he enables me to stand on the heights.
He trains my hands for battle;
my arms can bend a bow of bronze.
You give me your shield of victory,
and your right hand sustains me;
you stoop down to make me great.
You broaden the path beneath me,
so that my ankles do not turn.

Psalm 18:32–36

He who began a good work in you will carry it on to completion until the day of Christ Jesus.

Philippians 1:6

The LORD is good,
a refuge in times of trouble.
He cares for those who trust in him.

Nahum 1:7

He will keep you strong to the end, so that you will be blameless on the day of our Lord Jesus Christ. God, who has called you into fellowship with his Son Jesus Christ our Lord, is faithful.

1 Corinthians 1:8–9

*T*hose things we consider difficulties are often God's opportunities for our greater blessing. We must trust, believe, hope and continue to walk the path he has laid before us.

> May our Lord Jesus Christ himself and God our Father, who loved us and by his grace gave us eternal encouragement and good hope, encourage your hearts and strengthen you in every good deed and word.
>
> 2 Thessalonians 2:16–17

God Is With Us . . .
In Our Confusion

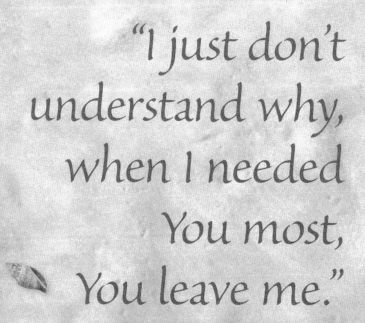

"I just don't understand why, when I needed You most, You leave me."

Many things in life cannot be explained: the death of an infant, the loss of a job, the rebellion of a child, the desertion by a loved one, or any number of circumstances beyond our control. Have you ever wondered Why did this have to happen? God can help us with those "Why?" questions.

Why do the wicked live on,
    growing old and increasing in power?
They see their children established around them,
    their offspring before their eyes.
Their homes are safe and free from fear;
    the rod of God is not upon them.

Job 21:7–9

Why, O LORD, do you stand far off?
    Why do you hide yourself in times of trouble?

Psalm 10:1

When times are good, be happy;
    but when times are bad, consider:
God has made the one
    as well as the other.

Ecclesiastes 7:14

"My thoughts are not your thoughts,
    neither are your ways my ways," declares the LORD.
"As the heavens are higher than the earth,
    so are my ways higher than your ways
    and my thoughts than your thoughts."

Isaiah 55:8–9

When faced with bewildering circumstances we are tempted to ask "Why?" But a better question to ask is "What? … What do you have in mind now, Lord?"

"Call to me and I will answer you and tell you great and unsearchable things you do not know," says the LORD.

Jeremiah 33:3

One thing I ask of the LORD,
*   this is what I seek;*
that I may dwell in the house of the LORD
*   all the days of my life,*
to gaze upon the beauty of the LORD
*   and to seek him in his temple.*
For in the day of trouble
*   he will keep me safe in his dwelling;*
he will hide me in the shelter of his tabernacle
*   and set me high upon a rock.*

Psalm 27:4–5

"As the new heavens and the new earth that I make will endure before me," declares the LORD, "so will your name and descendants endure."

Isaiah 66:22

*T*hough it may sometimes seem that things are out of control, we can take comfort in God's enduring promises and constant presence.

If … you seek the LORD your God, you will find him if you look for him with all your heart and with all your soul.

Deuteronomy 4:29

Jesus said, "All authority in heaven and on earth has been given to me. Therefore go and make disciples of all nations, baptizing them in the name of the Father and of the Son and of the Holy Spirit, and teaching them to obey everything I have commanded you. And surely I am with you always, to the very end of the age."

Matthew 28:18–20

"You will seek me and find me when you seek me with all your heart. I will be found by you," declares the LORD.

Jeremiah 29:13–14

"I the LORD do not change."

Malachi 3:6

You, O LORD, are a compassionate and gracious God, slow to anger, abounding in love and faithfulness.

Psalm 86:15

Who is a God like you,
*   who pardons sin and forgives the transgression*
*   of the remnant of his inheritance?*
You do not stay angry forever
*   but delight to show mercy.*
You will again have compassion on us.

Micah 7:18–19

His mercy extends to those who fear him,
*   from generation to generation.*

Luke 1:50

Our citizenship is in heaven. And we eagerly await a Savior from there, the Lord Jesus Christ, who, by the power that enables him to bring everything under his control, will transform our lowly bodies so that they will be like his glorious body.

Philippians 3:20–21

The Lord is good and his love endures forever;
*   his faithfulness continues through all generations.*

Psalm 100:5

God, who has called you into fellowship with his Son Jesus Christ our Lord, is faithful.

1 Corinthians 1:9

"I am bringing my righteousness near,
it is not far away;
and my salvation will not be delayed," says the LORD.

Isaiah 46:13

Blessed are you who hunger now,
for you will be satisfied.
Blessed are you who weep now,
for you will laugh.

Luke 6:21

God, who has called you into fellowship with his Son Jesus Christ our Lord, is faithful.

1 Corinthians 1:9

Put away all doubts. Cast out all confusion. Stand firm in the work of the Lord and find a renewed faith following in his footsteps.

Arise, shine, for your light has come,
and the glory of the LORD rises upon you.
See, darkness covers the earth
and thick darkness is over the peoples,
but the LORD rises upon you
and his glory appears over you.

Isaiah 60:1–2

God Is With Us ...
As Our Loving Father

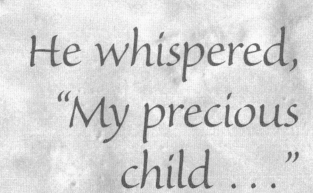

He whispered,
"My precious
child ..."

The Creator of the universe calls me his child—what a blessing! What a privilege! What a responsibility!

The LORD disciplines those he loves,
as a father the son he delights in.

Proverbs 3:12

"I will be a Father to you,
and you will be my sons and daughters,
says the Lord Almighty."

2 Corinthians 6:18

Endure hardship as discipline; God is treating you as sons. For what son is not disciplined by his father?

Hebrews 12:7

You are my Father,
my God, the Rock my Savior.

Psalm 89:26

To us a child is born,
to us a son is given,
and the government will be on his shoulders.
And he will be called
Wonderful Counselor, Mighty God,
Everlasting Father, Prince of Peace.

Isaiah 9:6

O LORD, you are our Father.
We are the clay, you are the potter;
we are all the work of your hand.

Isaiah 64:8

You did not receive a spirit that makes you a slave again to fear, but you received the Spirit of sonship. And by him we cry, "*Abba*, Father."

Romans 8:15

For us there is but one God, the Father, from whom all things came and for whom we live; and there is but one Lord, Jesus Christ, through whom all things came and through whom we live.

1 Corinthians 8:6

There is one body and one Spirit—just as you were called to one hope when you were called—one Lord, one faith, one baptism; one God and Father of all, who is over all and through all and in all.

Ephesians 4:4–6

The Spirit himself testifies with our spirit that we are God's children.

Romans 8:16

As children of God we can trust that our Father will provide for us.

Jesus said, "Your Father knows what you need before you ask him."

Matthew 6:8

Jesus said, "Which of you fathers, if your son asks for a fish, will give him a snake instead? Or if he asks for an egg, will give him a scorpion? If you then, though you are evil, know how to give good gifts to your children, how much more will your Father in heaven give the Holy Spirit to those who ask him!"

Luke 11:11–13

As God's children, our Father knows us by name and bestows on us certain rights, privileges and responsibilities.

Do not think of yourself more highly than you ought, but rather think of yourself with sober judgment, in accordance with the measure of faith God has given you. Just as each of us has one body with many members, and these members do not all have the same function so in Christ we who are many form one body, and each member belongs to all the others.

Romans 12:3–5

*This is what the L*ORD *says ...*
        he who formed you ...
"Fear not, for I have redeemed you;
        I have summoned you by name; you are mine."

Isaiah 43:1

"I will pour out my Spirit on your offspring,
        and my blessing on your descendants.
They will spring up like grass in a meadow,
        like poplar trees by flowing streams.
*One will say, 'I belong to the L*ORD*';*
        another will call himself by the name of Jacob;
*still another will write on his hand, 'The L*ORD*'s'*
        and will take the name Israel."

Isaiah 44:3–5

*Before I was born the L*ORD *called me;*
        from my birth he has made mention of my name.

Isaiah 49:1

*O*ur loving Father cares for us as a shepherd cares for his sheep. And we, his children, need to listen carefully to his voice and obey.

Jesus said, "The sheep listen to [the shepherd's] voice. He calls his own sheep by name and leads them out. When he has brought out all his own, he goes on ahead of them, and his sheep follow him because they know his voice. ... I am the good shepherd; I know my sheep and my sheep know me—just as the Father knows me and I know the Father—and I lay down my life for the sheep. ... My sheep listen to my voice; I know them, and they follow me."

John 10:3–4, 14–15, 27

Know that the LORD is God.
     It is he who made us, and we are his;
     we are his people, the sheep of his pasture.

Psalm 100:3

God Is With Us ...
Always!

"I love you
and will never
leave you
never, ever,
during your trials
and testings."

*W*e often make promises we can't keep. God isn't like that. God is faithful and trustworthy. When God promises never to leave us, he means just what he says. He's not going anywhere!

Do not forget this one thing, dear friends: With the Lord a day is like a thousand years, and a thousand years are like a day. The Lord is not slow in keeping his promise, as some understand slowness. He is patient with you.

2 Peter 3:8–9

May God himself, the God of peace, sanctify you through and through. May your whole spirit, soul and body be kept blameless at the coming of our Lord Jesus Christ. The one who calls you is faithful and he will do it.

1 Thessalonians 5:23–24

Jesus said, "See how the lilies of the field grow. They do not labor or spin. Yet I tell you that not even Solomon in all his splendor was dressed like one of these. If that is how God clothes the grass of the field, which is here today and tomorrow is thrown into the fire, will he not much more clothe you, O you of little faith? So do not worry, saying, 'What shall we eat?' or 'What shall we drink?' or 'What shall we wear?'... Your heavenly Father knows that you need them. But seek first his kingdom and his righteousness, and all these things will be given to you as well."

Matthew 6:28–33

The earth is the LORD's, and everything in it,
the world, and all who live in it.

Psalm 24:1

I will praise you, O LORD, among the nations;
I will sing of you among the peoples.
For great is your love, reaching to the heavens;
your faithfulness reaches to the skies.
Be exalted, O God, above the heavens;
let your glory be over all the earth.

Psalm 57:9–11

"My people will be filled with my bounty,"
declares the LORD.

Jeremiah 31:14

The living may know that the Most High is sovereign over the kingdoms of men and gives them to anyone he wishes and sets over them the lowliest of men.

Daniel 4:17

I am still confident of this:
I will see the goodness of the LORD
in the land of the living.
Wait for the LORD;
be strong and take heart
and wait for the LORD.

Psalm 27:13–14

God has shown kindness by giving you rain from heaven and crops in their seasons; he provides you with plenty of food and fills your hearts with joy.

Acts 14:17

"Even to your old age and gray hairs
I am he, I am he who will sustain you.
I have made you and I will carry you;
I will sustain you and I will rescue you," says the LORD.

Isaiah 46:4

I was young and now I am old,
yet I have never seen the righteous forsaken
or their children begging bread.
They are always generous and lend freely;
their children will be blessed.

Psalm 37:25–26

When it seems that life is whirling out of control, we can take comfort in God's sovereignty and power. He has everything under control. And he will work his will in every circumstance.

Do not conform any longer to the pattern of this world, but be transformed by the renewing of your mind. Then you will be able to test and approve what God's will is— his good, pleasing and perfect will.

Romans 12:2

Commit your way to the LORD;
trust in him and he will do this:
He will make your righteousness shine like the dawn,
the justice of your cause like the noonday sun.

Psalm 37:5–6

Many are the plans in a man's heart,
but it is the LORD's purpose that prevails.

Proverbs 19:21

I desire to do your will, O my God;
your law is within my heart.

Psalm 40:8

I know that you can do all things;
no plan of yours can be thwarted, LORD.

Job 42:2

"I am God, and there is no other;
I am God, and there is none like me.
I make known the end from the beginning,
from ancient times, what is still to come.
I say: My purpose will stand,
and I will do all that I please."

Isaiah 46:9–10

Jesus said, "Look at the birds of the air; they do not sow or reap or store away in barns, and yet your heavenly Father feeds them. Are you not much more valuable than they? Who of you by worrying can add a single hour to his life?"

Matthew 6:26–27

I know that everything God does will endure forever;
nothing can be added to it and nothing taken
from it. God does it so that men will revere him.

Ecclesiastes 3:14

The LORD Almighty has purposed, and who can thwart him?
His hand is stretched out, and who can turn it back?

Isaiah 14:27

Let the peace of Christ rule in your hearts, since as members of one body you were called to peace. And be thankful.

Colossians 3:15

[Your beauty] should be that of your inner self, the unfading beauty of a gentle and quiet spirit, which is of great worth in God's sight.

1 Peter 3:4

Aim for perfection ... live in peace. And the God of love and peace will be with you.

2 Corinthians 13:11

Grace, mercy and peace from God the Father and from Jesus Christ, the Father's Son, will be with us in truth and love.

2 John 1:3

*W*henever we hit rock-bottom, we can be assured of God's love and care. His encouragement breathes new possibilities into impossible circumstances.*

In you, O LORD, I have taken refuge;
let me never be put to shame;
deliver me in your righteousness.

Psalm 31:1

Those who trust in the LORD are like Mount Zion,
which cannot be shaken but endures forever.

Psalm 125:1

The LORD is with me; I will not be afraid.

Psalm 118:6

Taste and see that the LORD is good;
blessed is the man who takes refuge in him.

Psalm 34:8

We say with confidence,
"The Lord is my helper; I will not be afraid.
What can man do to me?"

Hebrews 13:6

The eyes of the LORD are on those who fear him,
on those whose hope is in his unfailing love.

Psalm 33:18

God Is With Us . . .
As Our Strong Provider

"When you saw only one set of footprints it was then that I carried you."

Our problems may seem overwhelming, but God's power is stronger than any obstacle we may face.

"I am the LORD, the God of all mankind. Is anything too hard for me?"

Jeremiah 32:27

"See now that I myself am He!
There is no god besides me.
I put to death and I bring to life,
I have wounded and I will heal,
and no one can deliver out of my hand," says the LORD.

Deuteronomy 32:39

God does as he pleases
with the powers of heaven
and the peoples of the earth.
No one can hold back his hand
or say to him: "What have you done?"

Daniel 4:35

Wealth and honor come from you;
you are the ruler of all things.
In your hands are strength and power
to exalt and give strength to all.
Now, our God, we give you thanks,
and praise your glorious name.

1 Chronicles 29:12–13

Jesus said, "With God all things are possible."

Matthew 19:26

The LORD is slow to anger and great in power. ...
His way is in the whirlwind and the storm,
*   and clouds are the dust of his feet.*

Nahum 1:3

I can do everything through Christ who gives me strength.

Philippians 4:13

Be strong in the Lord and in his mighty power.

Ephesians 6:10

LORD, you established peace for us;
*   all that we have accomplished you have done for us.*

Isaiah 26:12

Not that we are competent in ourselves to claim anything for ourselves, but our competence comes from God.

2 Corinthians 3:5

The Spirit helps us in our weakness. We do not know what we ought to pray for, but the Spirit himself intercedes for us with groans that words cannot express.

Romans 8:26

The LORD is the strength of his people,
a fortress of salvation for his anointed one.

Psalm 28:8

In the LORD alone
are righteousness and strength.

Isaiah 45:24

"I will strengthen them in the LORD
and in his name they will walk,"
declares the LORD.

Zechariah 10:12

The Sovereign LORD is my strength;
he makes my feet like the feet of a deer,
he enables me to go on the heights.

Habakkuk 3:19

"I have raised you up for this very purpose, that I might show you my power and that my name might be proclaimed in all the earth," says the LORD.

Exodus 9:16

Since God is our strong provider, we can be assured that he is in control of every aspect of our lives. He will prepare the way before us. He will never leave us. And he will provide our every need.

My God will meet all your needs according to his glorious riches in Christ Jesus.

Philippians 4:19

This is what the Sovereign LORD, the Holy One of Israel, says:

In repentance and rest is your salvation,
in quietness and trust is your strength."

Isaiah 30:15

Surely this is our God;
we trusted in him, and he saved us.
This is the LORD, we trusted in him;
let us rejoice and be glad in his salvation.

Isaiah 25:9

"Before they call I will answer;
while they are still speaking I will hear," says the LORD.

Isaiah 65:24

Jesus said, "If you believe, you will receive whatever you ask for in prayer."

Matthew 21:22

No eye has seen,
no ear has heard,
no mind has conceived
what God has prepared for those who love him.

1 Corinthians 2:9

I call to the LORD, who is worthy of praise,
and I am saved from my enemies.

Psalm 18:3

O LORD Almighty,
blessed is the man who trusts in you.

Psalm 84:12

Now to God who is able to do immeasurably more than all we ask or imagine, according to his power that is at work within us, to him be glory in the church and in Christ Jesus throughout all generations for ever and ever! Amen.

Ephesians 3:20–21

God who did not spare his own Son, but gave him up for us all—how will he not also, along with him, graciously give us all things?

Romans 8:32

Praise the LORD, O my soul,
and forget not all his benefits—
who forgives all your sins
and heals all your diseases,
who redeems your life from the pit
and crowns you with love and compassion,
who satisfies your desires with good things
so that your youth is renewed like the eagle's.

Psalm 103:2–5

You will keep in perfect peace
*   him whose mind is steadfast,*
*   because he trusts in you.*

Isaiah 26:3

He who trusts in the LORD will prosper.

Proverbs 28:25

Anyone who trusts in God will never be put to shame.

Romans 10:11

Jesus said, "Whoever drinks the water I give him will never thirst. Indeed, the water I give him will become in him a spring of water welling up to eternal life."

John 4:14

Our God is strong enough to carry us, but also gentle enough to enfold us in his loving embrace.

The LORD tends his flock like a shepherd:
      He gathers the lambs in his arms
and carries them close to his heart;
      he gently leads those that have young.

Isaiah 40:11

He will command his angels concerning you
      to guard you in all your ways;
they will lift you up in their hands,
      so that you will not strike your foot against a stone.

Psalm 91:11–12

LORD, you have assigned me my portion and my cup;
      you have made my lot secure.

Psalm 16:5

The LORD is my shepherd, I shall not be in want.
      He makes me lie down in green pastures,
he leads me beside quiet waters,
      he restores my soul.

Psalm 23:1–3

As our strong provider carries us over the rough places in our lives, he speaks words of peace and blessing to our wounded hearts.

The LORD bless you
and keep you;
the LORD make his face shine upon you
and be gracious to you;
the LORD turn his face toward you
and give you peace.

Numbers 6:24–26

May the God of peace … equip you with everything good for doing his will, and may he work in us what is pleasing to him, through Jesus Christ, to whom be glory for ever and ever. Amen.

Hebrews 13:20–21

At Inspirio we love to hear from you—your
stories, your feedback,
and your product ideas.
Please send your comments to us
by way of e-mail at
icares@zondervan.com
or to the address below:

inspirio

Attn: Inspirio Cares
5300 Patterson Avenue SE
Grand Rapids, MI 49530

If you would like further information
about Inspirio and the products we
create, please visit us at:
www.inspiriogifts.com

Thank you and God Bless!